I0518052

Postlude
to the
End of

J. PARKER MARVIN

EDITED BY LANCE ÜMMENHOFER

-First Edition

Publisher's Cataloguing-in-Publication Data

Marvin, J. Parker
    Postlude to the end of / written by J. Parker Marvin
    ISBN: 978-1-953932-28-0

1. Poetry: General 2. Poetry: American - General 3. Poetry: Subjects & Themes - Death, Grief, Loss I. Title II. Author

Library of Congress Control Number: 2024940994

Praise for J. Parker Marvin

"The devotional care of holding space for someone's life — the 'quantum relationship' of one's mother — as they actively die at home is a complex interaction of emotions, familial relations, cultural ritual, and the pervading atmosphere of the environment that supports the continuum of life-death. J. Parker Marvin openly shares with the reader the primacy of the encounter with his mother's unfolding passing. This poignant series of poems is a daybook chronicling a soul-searing fourteen-day meditation on impermanence and transformation and the 'gathering time contracts' of sustained grieving that continues in time and space. Sensitively equipoised language conveys the arrival of silence and stillness. This gorgeously wrought elegy meshes 'tangents ambivalenting' in sanctified and intimate attention."

-Brenda Iijima, author of *Presence* (University of Georgia Press) and *Bionic Communality* (Roof Books)

"When calamity breaks us, destroying perceptions — our held beliefs or, even, faith — we 'frantic amateurs over a dying' tend to try to write it out along standardized lines, believing, perhaps, they can force the disaster into the fold of the acceptable past's grammar. Impossible. Postlude to the End of, J. Parker Marvin's debut poetry collection, is an intimate, startling, and disturbing record of the poet's experience of their mother's death — rendered in language like no other. 'Underwritten by' the 'and' of relationships, the poet moves into the zone of death and the future that is loss — a space demarcated by ambient wordscapes of information overload (the heard, remembered, and received of medical terminology and the biblical), repeated utterances, and halting pauses. From this plane, Marvin weaves this focused, intensive discourse on the subjective experience the deaths of closely-held others have upon our bodies and minds. In this book, you will see how memories can unconsciously attack our concentrations; and know how the deads' faces and voices fade from our remembering grip. You will wonder — frustrated, confused, and scared — 'what/is the value of words' as you are 'cleav[ed] from images.' Those of us who have experienced such loss will find much of this familiar to memory, all the while having been incapable ourselves to put it on our own pages. Those of you who have not experienced this loss — with caution and care — will know what to anticipate, to a degree, from this — such a raw and emotional poetry. Regardless — we all need this book.

-Thom Eichelberger-Young, author of *BESPOKE* (St. Andrews Press) and *ANTIKYTHERA* (Antiphony Press)

for my Mother,
Ann Martha Marvin
(August 2, 1946 – July 17, 2021)

W/

am but dust and _ _ _ _ _:	Gen 18:27
to you handfuls of _ _ _ _ _ of the furnace, and let	Ex 9:8
they took _ _ _ _ _ of the furnace, and stood befo...	Ex 9:10
to receive his _ _ _ _ _, and his shovels, and hi...	Ex 27:3
the place of the _ _ _ _ _:	Lev 1:16
place, where the _ _ _ _ _ are poured out, and burn...	Lev 4:12
and take up the _ _ _ _ _ which the fire hath cons...	Lev 6:10
carry forth the _ _ _ _ _ without the camp unto a	Lev 6:11
take away the _ _ _ _ _ from the altar, and spre...	Num 4:13
gather up the _ _ _ _ _ of the heifer, and lay t...	Num 19:9

J. Parker Marvin

my Mother will die in 14 days

civil lights patches   pockmark sidewalk
          fear syllabus   underwritten   by   and

small   solar fades   after   midnight
rape of   visible   and   universe

      protect temporal   protect bodies   protect
                    noone   cares | is   departure after

and bodies   at rest   passivate
the pixel   moments   kept   in

                  cycles of memory   but somewhere
          else and   noone   asks for

Postlude to the End of

my Mother will die in 13 days

Mediation   eyes   closed   body still
Exegesis into   viscous   white   milk

                    Doubt-wandering   but   always   returning
                  Interiors   to   the formality   emptiness

Tonalities   restrained   for   neutral   purchase
Always   the   thinnest   coat   peeling

                    Time is   wet   when   permitted
                   Inside   time   is the   undercoat

Of   and   sits   like   waiting
Not   like   fluctuations   of wanting

J. Parker Marvin

my Mother will die in 12 days

     Flux   language   meaning   give birth
Ignore   want ignore   grammar   ignore

Verbing the   page is desecration
Waste   allowance   is darking light

                  .   Wait for   wait   with   wait
             Withoutness   not neglect   not shame

Whying always   was   wastetime whyness
Was   always   irrelevant posttoddler burnout

               Wilt language   is   the firstchild
                So   of course   hold on

my Mother will die in 11 days

Aperitif of new   ending   parental
Schism   slow fracture   of body

Diabetic leg diabetic   leg   diabetic
Kidney diabetic   kidney   diabetic   lessons

On impermanence   diabetic hands corrosion
Diabetic   fistula diabetic   ventilator diabetic

Temporary pacing   wire   diabetic sepsis
Amputation amputation   amputation   shock shock

Shock   introductory   lesson in   surrender

J. Parker Marvin

my Mother will die in 10 days

Rush colloid   bodies   are   gathered
Plaques   of emotions   flake arterial

The   mother   pieces   on   tables
Clottage   clones   of our   fictions

Repainting   repainting the   white room
The nothing   liquid   fills   nothing

Hands   cannot   the clear   blood
The eyes   mourn better   in

The   eyes   trigger   everything   in
The   eyes   the eyes the

Eyes the eyes   the   eyes
The   residue   of   a   moment

Postlude to the End of

[silence]

Old woman waiting in darkness is not my mother ::

shadow darkening ::

there is no space for the diabetic artifacts ::

the metal wheels and the cold squeak ::

there are things that I wait for when I find sections of black solitude
littered on the fringes of that reconstituted street of vague childhood ::

that space where each of us died until the dying was over ::

there is nothing familiar about silence ::

I step into her waiting or some dream of understanding ::

until I know my mother is gone ::

wAsh

that gathereth the _ _ _ _ _ of the heifer shall wash...   Num 19:10

shall take of the _ _ _ _ _ of the burnt heifer of p...   Num 19:17

put _ _ _ _ _ on her head, and rent her garm...   2 Sam 13:19

be rent, and the _ _ _ _ _ that are upon it shall b...   1 King 13:3

was rent, and the _ _ _ _ _ poured out from the alta...   1 King 13:5

himself with _ _ _ _ _ upon his face.   1 King 20:38

and took the _ _ _ _ _ away from his face; and   1 King 20:41

and carried the _ _ _ _ _ of them unto   2 King 23:4

on sackcloth with _ _ _ _ _, and went out into the m...   Esth 4:1

in sackcloth and _ _ _ _ _.   Esth 4:3

sat down among the _ _ _ _ _.   Job 2:8

J. Parker Marvin

my Mother died 4 days ago

Solidification :: sinking into :: the and
Of sorrow :: clustering moments :: moment

the without :: the unawakening :: the
Numb the numb the numb ::

Anonymous blankets in broken chest ::
Remainder :: reminder :: fading version of

Last face :: the eyes :: glass
The looking :: the silence the

Silence the silence the silence ::
Goodbye goodbye goodbye goodbye goodbye ::

my Mother died 5 days ago

Blank   sudden   white   page   gift
No   now   know   one   absence

                    Kiss   the cold   cheek   again
          Again   again   again   again again

Each time   cooler than ambient
Again   again again   again again

                    Waste   spent   time   revising tense
                        Ambient body   held   in   gray

The bag   the   cryptic   shape
Carrying   and departure   the   empty

                    Again again   again again again
                    Sit   cool bed   no imprint

That   is   memory car   gone
The   vacant   the held   the

                            Row   of   faces   the   wet
                    Eyes   and   heat   that   silence

More   than   silence   that heat
Heat heat heat   heat heat

                    Today   they   took the   bed

J. Parker Marvin

my Mother died 6 days ago

Loop   verse   deeping   into body
    Kidneys   and   toxins   and   failure

Twenty   years   diabetic   the   accelerating
The   struggle   the   seven days

            God   god   god   god   god
            Long   exhale   long   exhale stop

There were no   eyes   and
Glass   glass glass   glass   glass

                              Only   witness I   was the
            Greater silence   greater   silence greater

I could   not   hold   that
The   air the   breath the

        Nothing   could not   hold   the
              And   again   and   again   and

Again the   silence   the silence

my Mother died 7 days ago

The   ok   repetition   the   pacing
Moment   over   moment   that breath

                    Open   ended   duration   do   not
                         What   wanting if   this   and

Whisper   and   awaken the other
Thin   blankets   and   cool air

                              Match the body   the   hands
                         A coldness   days   old   white

So   irrelevant   now   this   white
So   irrelevant   now   this   white

                    So   irrelevant   now   this   white
                         Cheek   kiss   forehead   kiss   lip

Kiss   lip   kiss   lip kiss
Scent   of   body   scent   of

                    Cheek   Ash   forehead   Ash   lip
                         Ash   lip Ash   lip   Ash

Scent   of   wood   box   scent
So   irrelevant   now   this   white

22

my Mother died 8 days ago

Left   leg   and memory   stitching
    Anesthesia   shock   and after ventilate

Truth   and its absence   ventilate
Body   creep gravity waist   ventilate

    Breakthrough   pain   breakthrough pain shiver
        Her ::   her sudden   her   cold

Body into slurry   and   suffer
We   watch we   watch we

        Value of witness   becomes   hospice
           No one   is   there   but

Ativan Ativan   Ativan Ativan morphine
Gurgling breath   morphine   morphine   morphine

    When   the   body   stops   functioning
           No   breath no   breath no

breath   no   breath no   breath

Postlude to the End of

my Mother died 9 days ago

Brokenness appearance   memory   fidget viscous
Want   the   waking   blanket   under

                    Colloidal   eyes   hand   wipe   neurotically
          Material   fade   contact   fade mouth

The closed cracked   open and
The closed leak   witness   voice

      Another   impermanence another   impermeable another
       Erasure   erasure   erasure   erasure erasure

The error   of   everything   slowly
Body   in a   gray   bag

            And   already ::   what   is   face

J. Parker Marvin

my Mother died 10 days ago

Tangents ambivalenting   caucasian   smoke   glassy
Talk   keeps   happening   trimming of

The   borders cold   blanket   unafraid
Son   daughter   son   daughter   son

Sudden   dispersings   of   bodies outward
Pressures toxic eyes   silence   binges

No one holds the   tears
Duration   and   we   are   being

Seconds   of   emoting   is   not
Closure   ambient body   gray   sack

Stairs   and   collapse   are   exits
There   is   no   looking   back

Car   corners   no   time   no

my Mother died 11 days ago

Mentation   devolved   new   colds   ensconced
Border   composing   its   meaningless white

                  Is   and   actually is illusory
      And   more   relative   to   blanket

Over   pre-Ash   body   wait   for
Reclamation   do not   whisper at

      There   is   nothing   there   is
      Nothing   there   is nothing walk

Deliberate   trajectory   toward praying   subconscious
Is at   least   and similar

      To   the   and the end

J. Parker Marvin

my Mother died 12 days ago

Nights   since and   the   counting
    Of hours   and   breathing   and

Pacing   fear and   liquid pooling
Droplets   droplets the   clamming skin

  Repetition   collar bone   forehead   wrist
    Memory   is   similar this condensate

Fingers lips   fingers   lips   remember
Shivering   to   maintain   a   body

    Shivering   the   fan cold   over
      Cold   and again and   again

Silence over   silence   over   collar
Bone forehead wrist   fingers   lips

      Lip   lips   lips   lips   lips

Ash

are like unto _ _ _ _ _, your bodies to bodies o...   Job 13:12

like dust and _ _ _ _ _.   Job 30:19

repent in dust and _ _ _ _ _.   Job 42:6

I have eaten _ _ _ _ _ like bread, and mingled my   Ps 102:9

the hoarfrost like _ _ _ _ _.   Ps 147:16

feedeth on _ _ _ _ _: a deceived heart hath turned   Isa 44:20

sackcloth and _ _ _ _ _ under him? wilt thou cal...   Isa 58:5

them beauty for _ _ _ _ _, the oil of joy for mour...   Isa 61:3

wallow thyself in _ _ _ _ _: make thee mourning, as   Jer 6:26

yourselves in the _ _ _ _ _, ye principal of the flo...   Jer 25:34

29

Postlude to the End of

my Mother died 13 days ago

Ashes box   quantum   relationship   mother
Hospice   body   and   stillness   I

           There   was   witnessing   and   departure
                              There   was   a   voice and

There   was   a   voice   and
The   halting   sound   the gravity

                        A   mass   moved a   mass
                  Strapped   the tightening   that   tightness

Redefinitions   of   and   we   watched
The   door the   descent   the

                        And   we   were   and   distraction
                  The   car   was   gone   before   I

I   am told   the   Ashes
How   quickly   ambient   how quickly

                        Like memory   and   how quickly

30

my Mother died 14 days ago

A   mother and   relativity   displacement
Farther   away   farther away   farther

Nothing   is   the   slowing   down
This prediction   this and waiting

Is   the same   waiting   forward
Puddles   of   after   rivering   faces

I have seen   the elegant
The   manifesting   and   the equation

But   the   authors of   are
Not   we   did not   purchase

The   elegant   and   her Ashes
The   enclosure the   minimal   air

The darkness the sounding in
Of   course   we   wonder   of

Course   we   wonder   out   loud

my Mother died 15 days ago

Already redefinitions   the   looping   flows
Circle circle circle circle   circle

                              I   know   an approximation   of
                                    And I   was watching but

The time   came   after   and
The   time   came after   Eyes

                    Tracking   something   Eyes   open   and
                                    Eyes   full   full full   of

And   eyes   and eyes   and
Memory   of   grass memory of

                              Heat and   the silence   the
                    Prelude the   violence circle   circle

The   violence   of   late   sky
The   violence   but we   must

                    Not   talk   but   we must
                    Not   but   there are   and

We must   touch   after ending

J. Parker Marvin

my Mother died 16 days ago

Suddening   consciousness   akin to   falling
        Cluster   eyes   baryon   acoustic   oscillations

Observing   and there   was   interaction
Calming voice   intentions we   were

                Frantic amateurs   over   a   dying
        She   was   wasn't   and   still

Breath gurgling   and   there was
And her   voice kept   trying

                        Cipher   of   origin   and naked
            There were   eyes   and   beginning

There   were   hands there   were
And   old remnants and paint

                        And   we   were not   looking
                    And   we were   not   handing

Old stone   then old now
Old   always   stone   scope   of

                    Always   we   found   the   paint
                    In darkness   we   found   eyes

In darkness   cannot   see   cannot
See   cannot see   her   body

                        Was held   was   falling   was

33

my Mother died 17 days ago

Stone marker   returning weeds   lament
Artisans   faking   definitions   of   scripture

            Voice   wait over   Ashes   sink
            Pray   dirt   is body   memory

White the   carbon   and sorrow
The   face   the blankets of

              And   the   field is   not
           And it   is   not   empty

And the   field   stones itself
And the   field   and   voices

            And   the field   and the
        Field   and   this   is withoutness

The   dirt the   box   forgettingness
Shovel her   name toward mouth

        Shovel   her name toward   mouth
       Shovel her name   toward   mouth

Absence absence   absence absence absence
Ash   wood dirt and voices

        Ash wood dirt and voices
      Ash wood dirt and voices

Dirt   dirt dirt dirt dirt

J. Parker Marvin

my Mother died 18 days ago

                Neglect   forget   give the   want
         Mouth   give   into   want   voice

There   and the   is lost
The   was   eternal and   absent

               Press   against   her cool   pink lips
                   Not   too late to imagine

Corpse   body corpse body   corpse
The   hold the   release   the

               I know   I   was   public
           I   know   I   was repetition

It   is   the losing   losing
It is   burn   the   thin

        White   bedsheets   after   her removal
            After her   is   not pronoun

After her   is irrelevant walk
The   same   door   is   exit

        Walk again   and   the   want
         Walk   again   and   see   her

Ashes   Ashes Ashes Ashes   Ashes
Walk   again   and   see   her

my Mother died 19 days ago

Sifted   air   and   shadow   of
Grey   Dusting over   and the

                 Familiar   and   the dormant under
               And dumpster   over black   fade

Over   stains   already   and   afternoon
Of   the   rain   and of

               And   it resembled   violence   from
           And we remember   and   slivers

And   the sorrow   is   like
And   the   shade   and   the

               Repetition   and   everything nothing   and
           Why   are   the   endings of

And   why the   meaning   and
What   is   the   left   and

                   Where is that   lasting   of

J. Parker Marvin

my Mother died 20 days ago

Pressure   out   pressure   out   bloat
Of faces   the   release   of

Grief is   the moment relaxes
No   one   wants   to   sudden

Lack   of inbreath   sudden broken
Meditate   and find   the   pattern

No   one   wants to   inbreath
Absent   absent   absent absent   absent

I was   the one   who
I   was   the   one who

I   was the   one who
And my eyes   and   open

And exhale and   wait   and
No one   no one no

I   was   the one   who
Nobreath nobreath   nobreath   nobreath nobreath

my Mother died 21 days ago

Birth engravings   death   engravings   memory
A   'body forgets its   sweat

               Too   literal but   and   we
        Does   someone   remember   out and

Something   held the   of wait
And   tomorrow   and   tomorrow wait

             Collections   of blood   of   togethering
                It   was practice pressure   bodies

Tears of   tears   of was
Practice   no   one   or   asking

             No   one   revisions but rememory
               No   one   old   function   old

Bed no one   called   right
Sit   on   it after   chair

          And   conversations gap   the   of
And   conversations   revisions   of   tense

Everything   flow   uncomfortable   habit   the
Kiss   onto and   cold   skin

          The   kiss onto   cold   skin
             Kiss   the   cold   the skin

Kiss   cold   kiss   cold   kiss
Kiss cold kiss cold   kiss

          Kiss   cold kiss   cold   kiss
             Kiss cold   kiss cold   kiss

Kiss cold   kiss cold   kiss
Kiss   kiss kiss   kiss   kiss

J. Parker Marvin

my Mother died 22 days ago

The   in   the   direction   we
        Sever   of waiting   of   severe

We into   the   of against
We   and the   sincere   pattern

            Ofness and   absencing and   fraying
        Needle   discard for   droplets   excess

And the   becoming   and   the
Pooling   and   the   gurgle   breath

                    No   mute no mute   no
            Mute of   the   present   became

And too quickly   and   density
Air absent   body what   wilting

            And   we   are   of   definitions
                And   we   are of moments

Too   many books and   we
Lacking   eyes   definition   too   many

39

my Mother died 23 days ago

Tear   hand   cheek   touching   from
And her mouth   was   closed

                          Lightly   lightly the previous   and
                          Her   soft   flesh   her soft

Flesh   and the   last   aurality
The   last   slipping wind   of

                  Her   soft   mouth   the   slipping
                          And   her and   at   last

It was   the   and   after
Of   silence and   that heard

          Emptiedness   that   heard   of   absence
                          And   the eyes   were   mine

And it was   of and
It   was   that   definition   of

                          Over   and   I held and
                          I held   and   I   wanted

And   that   over   and   that
Ofness   and that   absentness   and

J. Parker Marvin

my Mother died 24 days ago

Becoming   this   is   and   loss
Or   and losing or   and

Loosening   or   and lost   or
Repetition   is   only possible   after

Or   or   or or or
Trauma   language   is simple absent

Is absent   is   different is
Silent   or re-   everything   that

Face   what   is   within what
Language or   what   or   what

Dark   is   and too   much
Vacuum   is and too   much

What forgets both   sides   of
Or   and   what   forgets that   air

And   it   was   the   openingness
And   it   was   her breath

And   it   was a   dissipation
Inhale inhale   inhale inhale   inhale

But you   cannot keep   it
But you   cannot   keep it

But   you   cannot   keep   it

41

my Mother died 25 days ago

Severance   of   bucolic   white   patterns
Dry   well poverty farm   patterns

                   Outhouse hollow   barns   rust   patterns
             Broken   stone   fence   weeds graveyard

Family   dirt family   road patterns
Memory   under   pavement   under   patterns

                      Face of   Ash   skips erosion
               Dilute   black   wettened   black   stain

WAshes   out   wAshes   out patterns
Commoning   of   name   of   lips

                    Givingness of voice of   quiet
           Present   empty   empty   empty   empty

Patterns over patterned   over   forgetting
Everything of   erasures of   mother

J. Parker Marvin

my Mother died 26 days ago

Of   Dust   humid Dust   years
        Of   memory of adherence   of

Molecules   of   breath   molecules   of
And we   look for   language

                    Bodies   are   made   of   Ashes
          Of   afterwards   of   molecules   of

And   we   look for and
We look for   and   we

                    Look for   and   we   look
          Of   discarded   and   steps   and

Carpet and weak wood   and
From each   is a   distance

                    From each is   a   silence
              Evolution allows   and   here   and

Truth   and here and   reinforce
The patterns   of   wheels   of

                    Her transport of   her   extension
              Of   her   machinations of   rust

And   the forgetting   is   pattern
And   do not do   not

43

my Mother died 27 days ago

Previous   of   gaps   previous   of
Fade   fade   fade   fade fade

                                        A   month   the   passing the
                              Almost   of   diabetic   of   binge

True   to   script   her   mouth
Our   mouths   and   no   remainder

                              Consolidate   the   pattern   dying   dying
                                        Of now   of boxes   of

Night   drunk   music   waiting   sleep
Morning   of symbols   of mourning

                              Body   strapped   tightly   tightly   tightly
                        Watch   the   strap tighten   watch

Mom mom   mom   mom   mom
Watch   the   strap   tighten   watch

                        Mom   mom mom   mom   mom

J. Parker Marvin

my Mother died 28 days ago

                Binged   weather first   night   of
            After   cleansing cleansing   electric   liquid

All   sound   of   release of
Is   there   misery   is   there

                            A   putting   out   of   posted
            Photocopy   refrigerator   protocol forgotten   days

Order of   cancellation   order   of
Do   not   of   body issued

                Decided   decided decided   decided decided
                    The   death   was   quicker than

And   the   waiting   of   witness
Of   time   of death before

                        But   it is   recorded it
                        Is   of   after   of writing

It   is   of   leaving   of
It is   of absence of

45

my Mother died 29 days ago

Broken   the cellular the   definition
I   recognize   the face   but

                    Of   want   of   memory   of
                        But   I   need the   picture

Of   quickness of erasure   Ashes
Of moment   of seeing I

                      And the   could notting we
                  Of   invisible   touch   the   skin

Wait   wait   wait   wait   wait
Of   a moment   of   knowledge

                    Do   we   know   the   whenness
                  Of a   body   of   how

What is this   of ending
What is   this finity   this

                    Stop stop   stop stop stop
                  The   asymptote   of body   bag

The   asymptote of and   the
Box   and   we must   carry

                  And   we must   the lightness
                  What will   it feel   like

To   cradle   what will feel
Cradle   cradle cradle   cradle   cradle

J. Parker Marvin

my Mother died 30 days ago

Corner   furniture   of   cherished items
Broken   broken possession   over   vision

It   is   of   the   must
Looping words her the   messages

Looping   pasts   her the   memory
The   after compilations   the   durations

Body   drunk toxins mind   resist
When we collected of   proximity

And the remnants   are   truth
Of   the duration of   weight

Of   body   and   passing   to
All   the witnesses all   the

And   moist   Dust layers us
Memory memory memory memory   memory

Cleanliness is loss   cleanliness   is
Of   salves   but   not salvation

Of   grasping   and   tangential   faces
And praying wAsh   empty   room

WAsh   empty   room   wAsh wAsh
WAsh   of   discard   of   gone

my Mother died 31 days ago

Abrasive   counting   of months   don't
And   one   and   one   and

                                             Of   no   the everything losing
                                                     Ands   losing ofs   losing

Messages   of   family becoming   textures
Zero   blankets   over each   face

                    Tangential   breaths   cannot   and   hands
                             And   reaching   and   only   bodies

Of   acquaintance and   the seeking
But   I want   the cold

J. Parker Marvin

my Mother died 32 days ago

Expectation weed   lily   exists   still
      Mothing over   old   chests   familiar

Smell of   wet antique   settlements
Of   memory   tumescent   field   broken

                Water   lives   in layers basement
      Brittle   under   broken   step   down

Step   down   muddy   tread tracks
Grown over   stacked   wheelchairs   and

              Piles   of   legs   obvious is
      Loneliness   in   old   attic boxes

Rot of   forgetting   this   forgetting
Cold   mothering cold   cold   cold

49

Postlude to the End of

my Mother died 33 days ago

Another   another   eviction not or
Request   breakingness and   the old

                              Furniture is   divided   and   no
                    One   and   the   wantingness   of

And that moment   and   that
Departure and what   is   division

                         And   is   word   and union
                         And   is union   of   disparate

And   is union   of   blood
Strangers   and   is pushing   into

            Broken   moments broken   moments   brokenness
                Scavengers   of   warm   kiss   kiss

Kiss kiss   kiss   kiss   kiss
Scavengers   are   better and   we

                         Are   not and   what   is
            The   new   definition   of acquaintance

50

J. Parker Marvin

my Mother died 34 days ago

Wall   thicken finger   of frozen
Reaching   and   I   held hand

But function   but nerves   but
Of   holding   her   then did

She   was   last   was empty
Moments are   suddenly   only   were

And   mine   what is   over
And   it   is   darkness and

It   is   but   the   moment
But   the watching   but   was

I   and   the eyes what
Was   the   of   seeing   what

Were   there did   she   my
And when   the   faces   overlapped

And we   imagine   binary   flickers
Did   she did   she   did

She   did   she   did   she

51

my Mother died 35 days ago

Rough cursive cheap frame memory
Corpse   pull through front   yard

     Animal burn   the   meat   instead
       Of arrogance of memorizations   of

Already   of   faded each renewal
Precedents of departure precedents of

     Regretting precedents   of we cleave
       From images we cleave   from

Voices of mothering the   isn't
We   keep we keep and

       Cold stone memory of   mothering

J. Parker Marvin

my Mother died 36 days ago

Evaporate   distillate   time   no   walk
Goes   a pace or   pattern

Seldom   name   seldoming   and   absence
Trauma   distance more   elastic   seeing

The   soon   will   soon not
And   coming will   lose   routine

Of   slackening   relation   the   blood
We   said   the   right   things

Shifting and   meaning   and   of
Habitual these   adhesions   what   is

Scarring   after   want the   hours

my Mother died 37 days ago

Faint   feignt fading   fadingness   body
In   a   room   in   without

                           The   weighting   of   a   box
                     Two   weeks   the   ground   the

Hold   the   gatheringed   the   pretending
Tears the   ripping   organics   collapse

                         Back   into   a   space grains
                  Of   presence   the   sifting of

The   sifting   into   the   sifting
We   postpone   the   public   sorrow

                         The   relative   the   stone   crops
                   No   water   no   purchase departure

J. Parker Marvin

my Mother died 38 days ago

                        Final   this   last   car   door
                        Rental   and   to   be   and

Returned   of   irrelevance tire   tread
Dirt   road   in memory but

                   And   memory   and   nothing   is
                   And   remember   and   eyes   and

Knotting   and   chest and   deep
And   deep   and   blindness and

                        Feel feel   feel feel   feel
                   And   deep   and   blindness   and

Feel   feel feel   feel   feel
Tactile   and   the   real   is

                        Memory and   the real   is
                        A   body a   body a

Body and   what   is   touch

Postlude to the End of

my Mother died 39 days ago

Distants diabetes   of   distortion   of
Mother complex   shunting   optional   the

                        Other bringingnesses of that memory
              Of   that and   only   deep

Staring   within durations   of   and
Couplets like   crippled fingers wanting

               To remember and   the   feeling
               Passes   and   the   hands   and

The   touch   but   what   is
And   eyes   and   feltness   and

               But   was   direction scalar   was
          Skin   touch   was   greater asymptote

Was   or was   or   was

J. Parker Marvin

my Mother died 40 days ago

Now   just   tiredness just and
Within the   every   of   subconsciously

And   there is   a   requirement
Deepeningness the   elongation   of   focus

Of   the   traumatic   of   remember
Of   white   sheets   over and

Of   white   body over   and
Of   and the   steppingness   of

And   the   outsideness   of   and
The   back corner   of   acre

And   just   staring   and   just
And   her   body and her

And   the   waiting and   her
Everythingness   and   is   all departure

Postlude to the End of

my Mother died 41 days ago

The   again   of   the   broken
You   under   and stand   with

                    Standard   dirt   standard   depth of
                    Shadowing   in   place   of   markers

She wanted   the   concrete   of
And   the   beautiful of   from

                         The beginning   mound marker
                For   density   for   slow   settling

And   it   is again   we
And   the must   of   passage

58

J. Parker Marvin

my Mother died 42 days ago

   Some words   meaning   lose of
    Think of repetition think   of

And it was her dyingness
And it   was her sudden

        Of Ash of   box of
    Ephemera touch   the pieces of

And   material is   without and
Origin   is not of foreign

     Suddenly the truth   of   made
     The holding   of the   ambient

The equality of the triviality
Of   and the   body was

      And the object of and
    Brokenness   into the   nothing of

Into the everything of   and
It is a choice and

     The memory of skins and
     Is there a weight to

And does memory   have mass

Postlude to the End of

my Mother died 43 days ago

Collections   attempt   the   renewal wait
Patterns   of   grieving   the   pale

                Whiteness did it   come or
    Memory   of   faded   the   blemishes

The aging   physical lag   of
Linear   equity of   senses crutch

      Bilateral   amputee   of understories   of
        Forget until   the zipper   the

Gray the   canvas   container the
Struggle   to   the   straps over

        The   missing the   shape   the
        Blunting toward she   became the

Weight of remain weight of
Remind   weight of remainder weight

J. Parker Marvin

my Mother died 44 days ago

Grief   redundant   family   chatter   texts
      The   father   relinquishing   the mother

Ashing the box   the   crumbling
Of memory of   familial   of

    Place dispossession the quick   happening
    The slowing   mind   the slowing

Message   departures are different   rewards
Do   not understand   the   running

    The   outages fire has always
    But   there is running   of

A   former   father charred face
Under   a   child   of   choking

    Of decades   there is   no
    Passage the   everything   of   gone

my Mother died 45 days ago

Peridot   match   of the   given
The   something   about   their   history

                              The   love   of   the not
                         But   blends   tend   to   and

Of   course   there was   no
Choice   look   into   look into

                         There   are   decades   but   in
                   The   beginning   they   could   have

In   the   beginning   there   were
In   the   beginning   hope   of

                    In   the   beginning   of   now
                         What   remnant and   I held

And   I   held   but   hands
But   skins   and   theories of

                    And   coldnessness   and   why not
                         Just make   up   and   what

Is   of   value   of words

J. Parker Marvin

my Mother died 46 days ago

Discussions   staccato memories tangent   pushing
                  Time   for time   for time

Agings   unfiltered   over   what are
And if   dead   things   mother

                  Over   and over   and   over
              Understand repeating   do   it   again

my Mother died 47 days ago

Shatter drones the full words
Of into empty blank it

          One word and of mutilation
        Or one word and Ashes

Or the blanket of threads
Mixed and into the blacknessing

            In a box again and
       Always of boundary of closing

Of   packing and down and
Soil oldening and organic and

      The physicality   of and   renewal
     We visit the nonemptinessed coordinates

Of soullessness of her of
We know   better than patterns

J. Parker Marvin

my Mother died 48 days ago

Stone   brochure   terminus   and   resemblance
Please accept   the   true   nature

Of   apology   another name   pictured
Permissioned   of   being   replaced   for

And gloss and   weight   and
Of   mechanized rehearsal   of preloaded

And   between   and difference and
Turning the   page   and turning

Decisioning the   edging   of and
There   is   only   the   naming

Stone   delivered   separately and   planted

Postlude to the End of

my Mother died 49 days ago

Downpour broken   river song   of
Driven   of   child   old   memory

          Destination   temporal lag of knowledge
          The   differentness   of   path   of

Arriving to witness the   dirt
Familial greetings   are   more   departure

          The   hoarding sadness   the vacant
          Is   obvious of   clinging   to

Body   relinquished   body   too   soon
Of   clinging   to   the   hoarding

          The heredity of the   fragility
             Of downpour of   broken of

River   of   song   of   releasing

J. Parker Marvin

my Mother died 50 days ago

Eventuality   and yes   it   and
Of   shovels of   scraping   of

Commencement   of and of   after
Bodies of   and the   unseen

The   collection   the   heirloom   gravity
What is   the   decomposition   of

And   we   have paid   and
Promise   and   we   believe   in   purity

And   what consumes the   Ash
Of   a   mother   body   and

67

Postlude to the End of

my Mother died 51 days ago

Water   the   transparent the   parent
Of   body   of   transition   of

                And   the   humidity   of   that
                              Room   and   the   fan   and

The   pause   of voice   of
Motion of   names   of   gathering

                                Of silence   of language of
                          Water   of   cooling of   flesh

Of   staring at   the   container
And   weeping of   staring   of

             Staring   of   staring   of staring
          And each   memory   has   containers

Of   a   darknessful room   of
And   remember and   touch   and

J. Parker Marvin

my Mother died 52 days ago

Salves   and   selves   the   wAshing
Of depth   of   shallowing   boxes

Of   approaching of   gap   of
And   it   is   these   summations

And   it   is these   breakings
Of prepaying of   arrangements of

There   is   dreading   there   is
Future there   is to   dread

Of   organic   of carbon of
Breathing   and someone will   bring

And   of   what are   what
Were   of   soil and moment

Of   the   ritual   and   worth

my Mother died 53 days ago

Gray patterns   of gray   vision
Of   fading   of fainting of

       Fleshing and   dimensions of a
          Box the waterlessness of body

Of gray Dust floating in
And we drink and   we

      And the gathering time   contracts
     The   jittering script   the   option

For forgetting   the ofness of
Home   the   andness of home

w/As

bodies, and of the _ _ _ _ _, and all the fields unto...   Jer 31:40

covered me with _ _ _ _ _.   Lam 3:16

themselves in the _ _ _ _ _: Ezek 27:30

will bring thee to _ _ _ _ _ upon the earth in the si...   Ezek 28:18

and sackcloth, and _ _ _ _ _: Dan 9:3

and sat in _ _ _ _ _.   Jon 3:6

for they shall be _ _ _ _ _ under the soles of your   Mal 4:3

in sackcloth and _ _ _ _ _.   Mat 11:21

in sackcloth and _ _ _ _ _.   Luke 10:13

of goats, and the _ _ _ _ _ of an heifer sprinkling   Heb 9:13

into _ _ _ _ _ condemned them with an o...   2 Pet 2:6

J. Parker Marvin

my Mother is dirt

Soil   brown   soil   gray   soil
Vinyl   box   plastic   bag   paperwork
Soil brown   soil   gray   soil

Dark   dark   dark   dark   dark
Dark   dark   dark   dark   dark
Dark   dark   dark   dark   dark
Dark dark dark   dark   dark
Dark   dark   dark   dark dark
Dark   dark   dark dark   dark
Dark   dark   dark dark   dark
Dark dark   dark   dark   dark
Dark   dark   dark   dark   dark
Dark   dark   dark   dark   dark
Dark   dark   dark   dark   dark
Dark   dark   dark   dark dark
Dark   dark   dark   dark dark
Dark   dark dark   dark   dark
Dark   dark   dark dark   dark
Dark   dark dark   dark   dark
Dark   dark   dark   dark   dark
Dark   dark   dark dark   dark
Dark dark dark   dark   dark
Dark   dark   dark dark   dark
Dark   dark   dark   dark   dark
Dark   dark dark   dark   dark
Dark   dark   dark   dark dark
Dark   dark dark   dark dark
Dark   dark dark dark   dark
Dark dark dark   dark   dark
Dark   dark dark dark   dark
Dark   dark dark   dark dark
Dark   dark   dark   dark   dark
Dark   dark dark   dark   dark
Dark   dark   dark   dark   dark

my Mother is dirt

Years and   days   ::   as expected
Routine is greater   than suffering   ::

Only   so   much   caring   in
Wavelengths::   the   flowing   outside of

Bodies   into   bodies into   bodies   ::
Loss   is   a thing   ::   supposedly   ::

But   they   say   that   of
Love   ::   and   they   is   nobody ::

And   they blanket   in   themes
Of darkness ::   and they   blanket   ::

And   the   elapsing   is   eyes   ::
The   staring   the   blanknesses   ::   empty

Is more   empty than   shallow   ::
There   is still   only   one

Song   ::   it   is how the
Eyes focus   and do   not ::

It is how   the   eyes
Dwell   in   spaces   of air

And   wait   for   a   dead
Face   :: and   wait   for   breaking

Invisibleness   ::   and wait   for hollow
To   leave   condensate   ::   or   leave

J. Parker Marvin

my Mother is dirt

Forevering the fiction of :: witness
Into the air shape :: witness

Into nights of stone :: witness
And you are knowing the

Mustness of :: the not white
Of and the of :: waiting

And this is how the
Nothings happen :: into ends of

And suggestions of regathering :: too
Weak for the promise :: too

Temporary :: too shadowed :: the parts
The parting :: death and divisions

And doubted it :: but it ::
A thousand pages of littered

Surface :: I forget where I ::
I forget I :: and again

We only know about displacement

Acknowledgements

My gratitude to the editors and readers of the magazines in which parts of this work were first published:

Audience Askew Literary Journal: my Mother Died 19 Days Ago

Mantis: my Mother Died 29 Days Ago

Waxing & Waning: my Mother Died 24 Days Ago; my Mother Died 25 Days Ago; my Mother Died 26 Days Ago; my Mother Died 27 Days Ago; my Mother Died 28 Days Ago

Punt Volat: my Mother Died 39 Days Ago; my Mother Died 40 Days Ago; my Mother Died 41 Days Ago; my Mother Died 42 Days Ago; my Mother Died 43 Days Ago

www.ingramcontent.com/pod-product-compliance
Lightning Source LLC
Chambersburg PA
CBHW011225120626
46545CB00010B/3151

* 9 7 8 1 9 5 3 9 3 2 2 8 0 *